poetry book #17
by
Elliot M. Rubin

Copyright Library of Congress
September 2020

ISBN - 978-1-7328493-9-6

No part of this book may be reproduced in any form whatsoever without the prior express written consent of the author.

This book is fiction, and all names, people, places, and happenings are from the author's imagination and are used fictionally.

Any resemblance to any living or dead persons and/or businesses, locations, or events is coincidental in its entirety.

All rights reserved

Dedication
To my grandchildren
Shane, Isabelle, Jonathan, Carter,
Alexandra, Melanie, Mollie, and Madison

In memory of my father
Herman S. Rubin
who wrote poetry all his life.

Preface

Poetry is to be read and understood. It is to be written in plain language for everyone's enjoyment. Too often, poets write in-depth, penetrating poems where you need to be well-read and versed in the nuances of literature to appreciate the poetry, not this book or any of my writings. I write so everyone can enjoy a few moments of intellectual satisfaction without consulting a dictionary or encyclopedia.

Table of Contents

dysfunction 8

love is gone and forgotten 9

redial 10

the club 11

my jill 12

root canal 13

i love to… 14

i miss her 15

out the door 16

creativity 2020 17

afraid to ask 18

daisy 19

a place in space 20

portland 21

why 22

sorry, this is terrible 23

watching 24

a killing virus 25

blue eyes 26

lonely grandparents 27

looking back 28

dance hall girl 29

differences 30

museums 31

one summer day	32
a day in june	33
colonoscopy	34
condolences	35
beer	36
x marks the spot	37
caring	38
decision	39
lovers	40
temptation	41
walking	42
beach vacation	43
for laura	44
memory	45
evening	46
dancing with the devil	47
an aging heart	48
tats	49
date night	50
#80 L Lane	51
real power	53
walking to the car	54
gambling	55
the dog	56

#2 W Lane 57

flower on the street 58

dysfunction

i remember holding hands
as we strolled
past the baled hay
on the farmer's field,
with the smell of dew
burning off
from yellowed, dry stalks
under an early morning summer sun

i don't smell it any longer-
flowers now have no fragrance,
perfumes sit on the dresser, closed-
your scent is missing,
long gone
from when we loved;
my sense of smell
disappeared,
when you did

love is gone and forgotten

i erased you from my memory.
you no longer take up important
space in my conscious mind-
the kisses we had disappeared
along with your loving hugs,
soft caresses, and gentle strokes
of my hair while i slept.
there is a new love in my life
to replace yours;
you are gone,
forgotten,
i erased you from my memory
never to be thought of again,
see!

redial

after many years
i called her to say hello,
seems her number changed;
someone else answered

i dialed from memory-
maybe i changed a digit or two,
she was enchanting;
we spoke for hours on end

we set a date for dinner.
a place where i often dined;
they have quiet booths
where we could talk undisturbed

except i forgot
to tell her the time-
i went to press redial,
but my phone didn't have the option

the club

tomorrow is like yesterday
yesterday is like last weekend
last weekend is like last week

i had enough of the stay at home club

my jill

she was my kangaroo lover,
bouncing back and forth
between her men,
not able to decide,
nor wanting to-
just having fun in
her land down under

root canal

this time
i could hear
the drill
as it comes closer,
picking up speed,
drilling through
my golden shield
that protected me
for many years;
yet surrendered
as she drilled down,
deep, then even deeper,
with thin, tiny steel fingers
reaching through the heart of things
into my innermost canal
till it found its mark-
killing my root,
killing my pain,
killing my marriage,
setting me free

to find real love

i love to...

i love to
mate,
copulate,
fornicate,
populate,
elucidate,
and educate,
a love date
before
it gets too late

because i go to bed
at eight

i miss her

as she stands in the doorway
her presence radiates,
heating the room like
the sun at high noon

charisma oozes from her smile
as she soothes ruffled feathers
of stressed and upset people,
bringing peace and beauty

today we pay our respects to her-
not from the pandemic we read about,
but the one that fell from
the headlines, opioid addiction

out the door

as a young girl, her stepfather
brought her upstairs at bedtime;
clutching her favorite doll
he covered her, then tucked her in

in more ways than one

wanting affection, she thought,
led her to date at a young age-
too many boys, too many men,
all for the wrong reasons

in middle age, saddled with
three kids, living in a welfare
hotel on the charity of others,
she finally looked in a mirror

she decided to get clean,
go back to school, allowing
her mind to leave the baggage behind;
she walked out the door without it

creativity 2020

when i hear a word or phrase
that catches my ear,
like a pretty girl does to my eye,
i write it down in my notes

later i roll the words over,
chewing them in my mind-
i taste the flavor of the sentences
until i blow out a sugary poem

like a large pink bubble
it pops, sticking onto paper-
stanza after stanza,
it's sweetness lingering

afraid to ask

at fourteen, my parents went to the catskills
dragging me along with my younger sister too.
i was seated at the teen table next to this girl
who was at least eighteen, voluptuous, blond,
and by desert placed her hand on my inner thigh

i was afraid to ask

at seventeen in high school, there was a
buxom student teacher in my english class
who always smiled at me, and would place
her hand on my should as she walked past

i was afraid to ask

at forty, i was attaching a hutch to a low buffet
while prostrate on the floor for a neighbor-
she laid close behind me, placing her arm
over my waist looking at what i was screwing

i was afraid to ask

at fifty, my wife and i were at dinner
with a couple who were workout nuts-
they invited us to go with them to the nude
beach at sandy hook national park

i was afraid to answer

daisy

bring me a daisy
bright and cheery,
brilliant yellow to
brighten my day

a place in space

in my worldview, there is space,
she met me in a familiar place-
we hit it off, cordoned our own space
others floated around, we stood in place

a few weeks later, she is in my place
my closet divided into our own space,
i'm thrilled she is in my home place
i have mine, she has a w i d e r space

i am so happy she lives in my place,
with her, i want to share my space
i love it when we kiss face to face

portland

i saw my fellow citizens protesting
on a river of black asphalt
while unknown
brown shirt secret police
in camo fatigues look on,
armed with deadly weapons
and masks kidnapping
innocent civilians,
whisking them away
in unmarked rental cars

a plank floats down the river,
i wrote my name on it,
as did the waves
of my brothers and sisters
marching behind me;
to mark our presence
before we disappear to
an unknown detention

the president learned well
from his russian puppet master,
as i watch our democracy
evaporate before my eyes.

why

why is it okay for you
  but not for me?
why is it okay for them
  but not for us?
why do certain laws
  benefit a select few
  but not the masses?
why do i need to live
  under your religious beliefs?

why?
 WHY?
  WHY!

sorry, this is terrible

i really don't like to write
with a deadline to finish by,
some say i'm really bright,
pick the pen up, i'd rather die

when i write, i'm such a sight,
i'd rather just go out to dine-
my words at times are such a blight,
especially with a glass of wine

the finished poem some say's fine,
to me, it's written with the ink of gloom,
my words all hear me whine,
my writings filled with hours of doom

sorry, this is terrible,
i'd rather write
something merrible! [sic]

watching

i like watching her
as she turns her head,
flipping long dark hair
onto gentle sloping shoulders-
noticing my stare
a smile appears
on her face, with
white teeth showing
behind sensual pink lips
i desire to kiss-
unfortunately,
some things in life
never happen;
except in my dreams

a killing virus

today we are dealing with a disease,
one of many which kill people, cutting
short lives of elderly, young, and in between
before their life should be ended naturally

there is a virus thousands of years old
still killing, maiming, and destroying people's
lives; racism and bigotry roar to life beyond
reason, logic, and facts to do its job of harm

blue eyes

your blue eyes are beautiful,
penetrating,
captivating,
with long hair
framing high cheeks

men love you
at first sight,
lucky you;
but i know
what they don't,
you're a miserable person
and a two-faced nasty bitch

lonely grandparents

the flowers don't bloom no more
sunday's are so quiet,
nobody comes to visit
as in recent years past

i miss hugs and kisses,
the squeal of children,
each day melds into another;
the flowers don't bloom no more

looking back

i remember my dreams-
so vibrant, with a life's goal
laid out on a bright path,
easy to follow, yet here i am

the way was so clear
in my mind when i started,
youth was my strength
nothing could stop me

as i near the end of my journey
i came close to my dream,
almost there, but life has a way
of derailing expectations

politics and recessions are
beyond my control, yet i landed
on my feet. comfortable in old
age, not regretting much in life

dance hall girl

he walks
out the door,
leaves behind
the greatest woman
he'll ever meet,
his loss

he found what he thinks
is true love
with a dance hall girl;
who lap dances
her way into men's lives
as a side piece,
making them think
it's the real deal

nothing wrong with it,
many do the same,
trouble is his kids
are left behind

losers never think about others,
only deal with their needs
of the moment

life goes on as usual

differences

upon reflection
i now realize
here is me,
there are them

in reality,
we are us!

in one world
living together,
let's get along
in peace

museums

i walk through the museum's
massive hallways
looking at art,
statues chiseled of stone,
costing millions
for people to gaze at;
in awe of the works
of monet, picasso, rodin,
many other artists
too numerous to list

there is another museum
where artists
use a different medium-
costs much less,
only a few dollars-
libraries are museums too;
authors sculpt and paint words
into poems, novels,
books stirring imaginations
or informing us
of so many things.
writers are also artists

one summer day

i was driving
on country back roads
when i pass
a small idyllic lake-
calm water,
lily pads floating,
two young boys,
(friends i think)
one black,
one white,
standing next to each other
on the shoreline fishing
and laughing, while
casting their lines out
onto the water
making gentle ripples
on a serene, peaceful day-
while the rest of the world
is in chaos;
killing each other,
terrorist bombs,
wars all over,
children dying,
starving,
death and destruction;
while two boys
enjoy a summer afternoon
at a small forgotten lake
in the middle of nowhere

a day in june

walking on the boardwalk
in asbury park,
the sun beats down
breaking everyone's spirit,
shirts absorbing sweat,
staining them
as if they came out
from swimming in the ocean

beads of water flow down the neck
of the young woman walking with me,
glistening against her skin,
streaming down her chest,
tempting me to dry her off
earlier, rather than later,
when we go back to our apartment

we pass the games of chance
hearing them hawking to us
try it, win a prize

i already won the prize being with her

praying when i cash in my tickets,
at my age, i live to tell about it

colonoscopy

as the lady in waiting
wheels the old knight
in to the procedure,
his arm has the
intravenous dagger
pumping saline,
waiting
for the sleep poison
to begin its work

the proud knight
is flat on his back
wearing a thin cotton gown,
barely covering the crown jewels,
his armor stored away-
a prepubescent looking
fair maiden gently flips him over,
exposing to all that which rarely
sees sunlight,
the drawbridge to the castle gone,
enabling it to be breached,
throwing a once-proud demeanor
into the castle's moat,
to be eaten by crocodiles and piranhas
who live in his fertile mind-
knowing the soft hands of the
princess nurse
will never touch him again

to his chagrin,
and her good luck

condolences

what do you say
to someone who
lost their spouse
of seventy years?

there are no words
you can offer
to ease the sorrow
or dry the tears

although the english
language borrows,
then incorporates,
foreign words as its own
it still lacks the right words

how can you console
the inconsolable?

beer

walking along
under a thick canopy
of tall, lush trees
on a heavily wooded
country road,
i notice on the side,
resting amongst tall uncut grass,
an empty, discarded beer can-
its contents consumed,
i suppose,
by someone driving past
that opened a window
to toss it out-

who would litter, despoiling
a bucolic place?
how many beers did the person drink?

around the next bend,
i saw a car waiting to be towed away-

waiting

with its front end hugging
a massive tree;
the airbag deployed, stained with dried, brown blood,
beer cans covered shards of glass

it is karma, i guess,
nature had its revenge

x marks the spot

when i walk around my home
i see the x on the floor
where she stood,
then said goodbye,
walking out of my life

gone…

we loved each other,
but society condemned us

different;
religions,
skin color,
parental views

too much
to overcome

we both married others
yet we meet every night

consummating our love
while we are asleep

                    a continent apart

caring

tonight
i saw a boy
who stutters
tell of his moment
with joe biden,
how one stutterer
tried to help another
learn to speak,
with tricks
by marking a paper
before reading it

tears filled my eyes

decision

they sat in the car
arms entangled,
lips meshing,
emotions intermingling
among words of love

last night
she spent kissing
another

he wanted more,
her bounty-
she is hesitant,
a decision
not easily given

he doesn't know
she is torn between
two loves,
which one will she
gift it to?

once given
not retrieved,
ever

who will be first?

him,
or
her college girlfriend?

lovers

Karen waited for her lover,
Eager to welcome him in,
Gently guiding, moving,
Elevating her hips,
Locking him in with a squeeze

temptation

sugar-laden swirls of sweetness
enveloped gently rounded curves
of yeast-baked goodness,
drippings pooling on the pan,
waiting for thick chocolate icing
to set, holding crushed
peanut butter cups on top,
nestled amongst
dark chocolate nougats

all i want is one donut,
one damn donut,
while she calls me
to hasten to the bedroom
to feed her desires

walking

on vacation,
walking with my ten-year-old grandson
on a resort barrier island, we stop
to admire the quaint homes
across the street

asked to describes one home
he tells me it's color, how tall it looks
and the small bushes in front

then i begin to tell
how the home is different
from the others near it-
it's color scheme
is unique,
the house is set back
more than the others;
besides having no awnings
as its neighbors do

i explain how this mimics life-
people are different, yet
have to live near each other
respecting everyone's uniqueness
regardless of how they look

beach vacation

how much cancer soaking skin
can we afford to expose
after slathering on lotion?
it is so illogical

people traipse around,
frolicking on hot
sand nearly
naked--
sweating,
vowing
to come back again
next year

this is fun?

i'd rather sit
in the shade
on a soft chair,
on a portico,
sipping piña coladas
watching everyone
running around
almost nude,
then come back again
next year
to watch them

to me,
this is fun!

for laura

spent lots of time
searching rubies,
blue sapphires,
emeralds
and diamonds;
different shapes,
sizes, colors

trying to find a perfect diamond
is an almost impossible task

then i found you

memory

her soft hands
gently touched
my cheeks,
pulled me
close to pink
luscious lips

my heart longs
for her love
and smile causes
hard men to
melt like butter

when i remember
her again, it hurts-
my heart broke

she left me for
another love

evening

out early in the day
working my tush for pay
there's this i want to say
i love you every day

working my tush for pay
when i'm home after work
listening to the jerk
saying do it his way

there's this i want to say
can't wait to end the day
to make love every way
because you are my bae

i love you every day
there's this i want to say
working my tush for pay
out early in the day

to love you this evening

dancing with the devil

she loved him completely,
with fervor
never
before experienced-
tonight on white sheets
the slow flow of red pooled
by her wrists, two deep cuts
end her sorrow, heartbreak-
his promises empty,
meaningless; he played her
as he did other girls,
who danced with the devil

an aging heart

sitting next to my wife, there
on the window ledge is a
dead fly on its back, legs up-
it's a death omen i thought

her chest is visibly heaving
as she gasps for air, oxygen
pumping through plastic tubes
as the end of life nears

we were, as kids, young lovers
who knew we were meant to be-
nothing could stop us being together
not parents or religous figures

nobody knows this; after
she passes i'm going home
to be with her forever-
i can't live without my love

tats

after a few dates,
we had some drinks
one stormy night
in my kitchen

the booze hit us-
while the wind blew
we kissed and hugged
ending in bed

i saw all her
tats on a body
i longed to love,
thanks to a storm

it raged outside,
it raged inside,
my heart raged
beating so fast

i discovered
my name tattooed
on her left chest-
she stayed forever

date night

saturday night, i'd pick you up;
we'd go to the drive-in movie
then sit in the back seat snuggling,
waiting for the screen to come alive

the film flickered
with music and words blaring
from a box hanging on a window;
all of them no distraction

marriage, kids, a home
with a white picket fence
we still were in teenage love,
it never stopped for us

love comes in many forms,
caring, kindness, soft touches,
sometimes it lasts a lifetime
starting on a date night years ago

CHANNELING BUKOWSKI

#80 L Lane
on afternoon walks
as i approach his house
i know he's sitting outside
on a folding chair
by his open garage door,
smoking what started
as a cigar is now a stump
of an expensive cuban stogie

the stale smoke floats in the air,
i smell it a block before i reach him-
he nods hello as i pass;
i give a short courtesy
wave of my hand, then keep walking

he reminds me
of irving the litvak
from my youth;
a brooklyn cab driver
with cigar breath, and
a thick guttural
Nuu Yawk City accent,
whose voice was impacted
as it traveled through
smoke encrusted vocal cords
straining to be heard

#80 was always there,
every day at three,
like clockwork, he'd nod,
i'd wave, then keep walking

we never spoke.

today i passed his garage;
the door is closed,
the folding chair is gone,
the lingering smell
of smoked cigar ash
still rising
from the front lawn

the only reminder he existed

real power

driving by some hookers
walking on the street
dodging oncoming cars,
they own all the things
they need to survive
to make money from men
who decide to take them
on a short date

money changes hands
between consenting adults,
in the privacy of a car
with tinted windows
parked on a side street

the women are all sizes,
they possess
a hidden
money-machine
making clients
powerless
to resist them

walking to the car

left work
on a warm spring day
walking to my car,
parked in a residential area,
there are three women
standing on the corner
by a chain-link fence
in front of a home, everyone
knows is a red-light house

as he approaches them
they open their jackets
asking if he's thirsty-
exposing three sets of
bare breasts;
most are sagging,
veiny, empty-looking,
after years of men partaking,

too bad for them
he's not interested

before leaving work
the seventeen-year-old
salesgirl closed the shop
then undressed in the back

now satiated,
the old hookers
have no appeal

gambling

i like playing the horses

those mighty beasts
with toned muscles
racing around an oval track
with their mane flopping
in the wind

with each powerful hoof beat
kicking up dry dirt
while a puny little man
holds on for dear life

he's gambling he won't fall off
or be trampled by the other horses;
while i gamble two bucks
the son of a bitch holds on to win

the dog

he lumbers onto
my homely looking
neighbor ellen's lawn-
a large dog
with spots of gray islands
on his black fur-
old, tired, too many joint pains
to run around any more,
no chasing cats
or mailmen,
kind of a dog's retirement

finding a spot
in the shade
under a tree
he lays down
enjoying a slight breeze,
then begins licking his genitals
as i'd like ellen to do to me,
if both of us were drunk enough

#2 W Lane

she spoke in circles
often repeating herself,
saying things over and over
while her husband
gently reminded her
she already said that

frail, sitting on a beach chair
in the shade inside her
open garage door,
a live-in caretaker
sits behind, just in case-
i'd often stop to say hello
to the three of them

friendly people with a lifetime
of stories to tell; their ending
approaching, i'd always listen,
then say goodbye to continue
on my walk- the next day
everything would repeat itself
as if it never was said or happened

this morning i looked out
my kitchen window-
a dark-colored van parked
in front of her home-
two men took in a stretcher,
then came back from the house,
a long black bag
resting on it,
looks almost flat,
like the frail old lady finally
finished telling her stories

flower on the street

on my daily
early morning walk,
i notice
a striking flower
on soiled
black asphalt;
its inherent splendor
caught my eye

lush,
soft,
petals of lavender and pink
spread out
laying helpless,
seems to give up on life

waiting

for something
to destroy its beauty

reminds me of yesterday
as i drove
by a bus stop.
i notice
a homeless woman
sitting alone,
possessions between her knees,
waiting to die
with no future,
watching life flee past

on black asphalt

Other books of poetry by Elliot M. Rubin

Scrambled Poems from my Heart
A Boutique Bouquet of Poems and Stories
Rumblings of an Old Man
Surf Avenue Girl - semi episodic poems
Flash Pan Poetry
Unrequited Love
Aliyah - an Episodic Memoir
My Life if I Took a Different Path -
      an Episodic Memoire
Bent Twigs and Wet Feet
Stories of the South - semi episodic poems
Selected Poems by Elliot M. Rubin
Chains of Love and other Poems
Cookies and milk with poetry
Paper + pen = poetry
Love Balcony and other poems

www.CreativeFiction.net

follow me on Instagram at

Elliot_M_Rubin
humanist poetry

www.ingramcontent.com/pod-product-compliance
Lightning Source LLC
Chambersburg PA
CBHW060858050426
42453CB00008B/1011